Marimba 1

SOLDIER'S MARCH
from *Histoire du soldat*

Marimba 2

SOLDIER'S MARCH
from *Histoire du soldat*

Igor Stravinsky
transcribed by Murray Houllif

Vibraphone 1

SOLDIER'S MARCH
from *Histoire du soldat*

Igor Stravinsky
transcribed by Murray Houllif

♩ = 112

Vibraphone 2

SOLDIER'S MARCH
from *Histoire du soldat*

Igor Stravinsky

transcribed by Murray Houllif

Xylophone 1

SOLDIER'S MARCH
from *Histoire du soldat*

Igor Stravinsky
transcribed by Murray Houllif

Xylophone 2

SOLDIER'S MARCH
from *Histoire du soldat*

Igor Stravinsky
transcribed by Murray Houllif

SOLDIER'S MARCH
from *Histoire du soldat*

Igor Stravinsky
transcribed by Murray Houllif

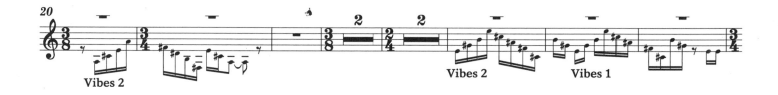

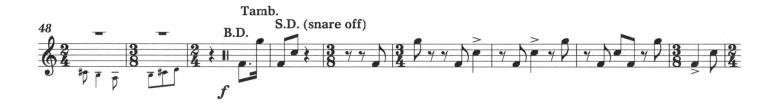

IGOR STRAVINSKY

SOLDIER'S MARCH
from *Histoire du soldat*

Arranged for Percussion (or Keyboard) Ensemble

by Murray Houllif

(Score and Parts)

ED 4022
First Printing: August 1997

ISBN 0–7935–7309–2

G. SCHIRMER, *Inc.*

DISTRIBUTED BY

HAL•LEONARD®
CORPORATION
7777 W. BLUEMOUND RD. P.O. BOX 13819 MILWAUKEE, WI 53213

PREFACE

Histoire du soldat is a chamber play for two actors, a dancer, and a narrator, composed in 1917–18 by Igor Stravinsky and the Swiss novelist C. F. Ramuz. It was first performed in 1918 in Lausanne. The percussion part was first performed by M. Jean Morel, who later taught at the Juilliard School of Music.

Stravinsky's incidental music consists of 11 concert pieces and 5 short cues. The "Soldier's March" opens the work with its acrid dissonances and pungent rhythms. The bass part (marimba 2) plays a "left-right, left-right" marching accompanying figure throughout most of the piece. Fragments of the marching tunes are passed from one instrument to another and then sounded by all of the instruments, *tutti*.

The percussionist should stand and may find it desirable to suspend the tambourine from a cymbal stand. Mallet selection is at the discretion of the performer(s) and the conductor.

—Murray Houllif

duration: ca. 2 minutes

The original instruments are indicated on the first page of the score,
in parentheses, below the mallet instruments names.

SOLDIER'S MARCH
from *Histoire du soldat*

Igor Stravinsky
transcribed by Murray Houllif